Books and their Authors

A book

by Jonquil Freedman

and Dan Freedman

"Don't Do It"

By

Yul Regretit

"Digging for Gold"

by

Annie Luckyet

"I Dare You"

By

Will U. Dewitte

"Archeology"

By

Barrie Dunderground

"How to Read The Weather"

by

Sunny Showers

5

"Locked Out!"

By

Lucy Keyes

"An Analysis of Opera"

by

O. Solly Mio

"Be a Responsible Team Member"

By

Carrie Myonwate

"How to Rob A Bank"

By

Casie Joint

"Pit Mining Techniques"

By

Doug Abighole

"Compulsive Dieting"

By

Wade Everyday
and Ann Orexic

"Plastic Surgery"

By

Abbey Gnose

"Sugar Free Cooking"

By

Less Tastystuff

"Back To School"

By

Don Myhomework

14

"Moon Phases"

By

Wayne N. Waxin

15

"European Restaurant Reviews"

By

Francis Best

"Comedy Routines"

by

Joe King

"2000 Years of Religion"

By

Chris Chin

"Cave Formations"

By

Chris Talls

"Crossing the Chasm"

By

Will Youjump

"Vegetables I Know and Love"

By

Carrie Tonbok-Choi

"How to win an Election"

By

Paul Itix

"A Review and Guide to Public Toilets"

By

I. Peter Write

"Proposal Techniques"

By

Mary Minnow

24

"Weather Reporting"

By

Gail Windygusts

"Back from my trip"

By

Jim Ismee

"Gossip"

By

Ann Sohesaid

"Math and Grammar"

By

Ed Jucation

"The Road Trip"

By

Harvey Thereyet

"Protect Yourself Against Bullies"

By

Lee Vussalone

"Writing Instruments
of the Modern Office"

By

Marcus N. Pens

"Offshore Angling"

By

Bill Fish

"Simplify Your Life"

By

Sally Tall

"Causes of Lung Cancer"

By

Sig Oretz

"Gourmet Cooking"

By

Dee Lishus

"Credit Cards for Everything"

By

Bill Melater

"After the Merger"

By

Riece Tructuring

"Interesting Hobbies"

By

Ben Therdon That

"Marsupial Baby
Transportation"

By

Joey Pocket

"Celebrity Parties"

By

Willoughby Coming

"Let's Hope It Works Out"

By

Bess Tovluk

"Don't Let It Boil Over"

By

Lydia Cookpot

"How to Make a Profit"

By

Jack Updiprice

"Save the Environment"

By

Less Industry

"Aging Gracefully"

By

Oliver Longtime

"An analysis of Star Wars"

By

Jed I. Nite

"Harassment at Airport Security"

By

Pat Medown

"My Time On Wall Street"

By

Robin M. Blind

"Food Poisoning"

By

Ralph N. Feelbetter

"How To Make Money

On Lawsuits"

By

Sue L. Parties

"Why She's Alone"

By

Herman Lefter

"The Most Profitable

Movie Genre"

By

Horace Tory

"Blunt Explanations Are Best"

By

Hester Thing

"It Was a Big Surprise"

By

Hugh Musbie-Kiddin

"The Spoils of War"

By

Victor Takesem

"So, Now You're Retired"

By

Lester Getdun

"Christmas Carols"

By

Joy Tuderwold

"Why I Had a Car Accident"

By

A. von Vaystreicht

"Public Schools Today"

By

Helena Handbasket

"The Long Engagement"

By

Willie Marie Yu

"My Time
as a Carpet Installer"

By

Walter Wall

"What to do
When The Pilot Dies"

By

Yolanda Plane

"It's Been a Long Day"

By

Yvonne Togohome

"Happiness"

By

Zeke Eetolyf

"Elementary Spicing Recipies"

By

Zoltan Peppa

"Romantic Transportation in Asia"

By

Eric Shaw

"The Worst Journey
of My Life"

By

Helen Back

"The Unexpected
Wedding Guest"

By

Harold Boyfriend

"Becoming a Supermodel"

By

Imogen Print

"Chinese Mail Order Brides"

By

Hymie Luvyoumor

"Christmas Gifts
for Corporate Wives"

By

Jules R. Best

"World's Hardest Puzzles"

By

Jeff Igritout

"What To Do When The End Of The World Comes"

By

Jethro Aparti

"Attacked By Wild Animals"

By

Wolfgang Torimup

"Destroy The Evidence!"

By

Bernie Tall

"World's Longest Poems"

By

Boris L. Totears

"Unbelievable Stories"

By

Candice B. de Fact

"Modern Medical Research"

By

Gene Eticodes

"The Utilitarian Principle"

By

Gretta Good

"Say Hello In German"

by

Gordon Targ

"Why I Can't Save Money"

By

Spencer Lot

"The Sure Thing"

By

Cindy Bagg

"Reporting a Crime"

By

Nevil I. Tuplice

"I Lost My Balance"

By

Ilene Dover and Phil Down

"Fun with Math"

By

Adam Up

"Airplane Crashes"

By

Yolanda Wong

12660799R00055

Printed in Great Britain
by Amazon